Critical Thinking Skills

Tools to Develop your

Skills in Problem Solving

and Reasoning

Improve your Thinking

Skills with this Guide

(For Kids and Adults 2021)

Nadia Fuller

Table of Contents

Introduction

Congratulations on purchasing *Critical Thinking,* and thank you.

Critical thinking has been on people's mind since time immemorial. Throughout history, philosophers have focused on what constitutes rational or critical thought, and they have developed a process to allow for it. Socrates, an ancient classical Greek philosopher who is believed to be one of the founding fathers of philosophy as we know it, was focused on critical thinking during his lifetime from 470-399 BCE. He focused on how to think, understand and rationalize, crucial skills in critical thinking.

When you learn how to think critically, you can understand the world around you better. You are able to examine any tidbit of information that comes your way in a way that is unbiased, informed and practical in order to determine whether it is trustworthy or biased. In so doing, you can decipher between something being a valid thought, belief or assertion.

In life, critical thinking can be useful to parse between real and fake news, to tell whether a person is lying about something or whether a conversation is worth your time and attention. Once you master the art of critical thinking you can solve problems, choose right from wrong and prioritize a to-do list in order of urgency and importance. It extends throughout other aspects of life, whereby you're able to make good and reasonable judgments based on the information provided, as well as able to take out any information that does not matter to you.

As you read this book, you will get a brief introduction to critical thinking— as well as discover the core critical thinking skills. You will get a glimpse of the qualities a critical thinker, contrasted with the behaviors of a non-critical thinker. Additionally, you will learn about the benefits and obstacles of critical thinking.

You will get steps to prime your body to be a critical thinker, and guidance through the process of critical thinking. On top of all that, the importance of raising a critically thinking child, as well as how to ensure that your child develops those important skills. Finally, you will be provided with several exercises that will help to boost your own current critical thinking skills.

Thank you once more for choosing this book despite the pool of choices. Every effort was made to ensure it is packed with useful and educative information. Please enjoy!

Chapter 1

What is Critical Thinking?

Imagine that you are at home with your four young children aged 7, 5, 3 and 5 months old. They are all currently crying, and you need to figure out in what order to help them—the infant is crying because she has a dirty diaper, and it is time for her to drink her milk. The 7-year-old is crying because he jumped off of a desk, hit his head, and is bleeding. The 3-year-old is crying because the episode of his favorite television show has ended, and you need to go select a new one for him, and the 5-year-old is crying because she says everyone is too loud and her head hurts. Who do you take care of first?

7 year old boy
•Crying becuase he is hurt and bleeding after hitting head

5 year old girl
•Crying because she has a headache from all the crying of her siblings

3 year old boy
•Crying because he wants more television

5 month old girl
•Crying because she has a dirty diaper and is hungry

It can be hard to figure out the best way to juggle the chaos in your home at that moment—you have a child bleeding profusely, a child with a headache, a child who wants help with something relatively unimportant and an infant in need of a diaper change and nursing, requiring you to stop and sit down for at least 20 minutes. You could do things by age—working from the youngest up to finally helping the oldest with his head injury after meeting the needs of everyone else, or you start with helping your oldest first then the younger ones. Ultimately, you need to figure out the best order to handle everything in a reasonable manner that leaves everyone happy and well taken care of.

Critical Thinking

This is where critical thinking comes in and you are able to gather information quickly— look around that room filled with sobbing children and figure out exactly why everyone is crying in an instant. After which, you can start begin to solve the conundrum in order of most to least important—in this case, it is most likely going to involve you first checking on the child who is bleeding to make sure it is not severe enough for a hospital visit and getting him all patched up, so he is not getting blood on everything. After which, you would most likely change the diaper of the baby, then fix the television before settling down to feed the baby.

Doing this then directly solves the 5-year-old's problem since she was bothered by all the crying, and once you have tended to everyone else and solved all of their reasons for crying, you calm her down as well. Suddenly, you are sitting in a room with four happy children, all thanks to your ability to handle the situation rationally.

Notice how, the whole process was guided by a set of steps, like you first assessed the situation— gathered all the necessary information. Then, you were able to conceptualize it—everyone is crying for a reason, and they are all distinctly separate problems. You are then able to analyze by importance— first and foremost you need to make sure that the oldest child is not severely injured because severe head wounds can warrant emergency room visits. Then, you need to ensure that your infant does not sit in a dirty diaper that could lead to a rash. At that point, you still have an infant that needs to be fed, but doing so will leave the other two children endlessly crying until you finished, so you take the thirty seconds to fix the television. It made the most sense to fix the show then because doing so will ensure that the middle two children stop crying, and really your infant waiting an extra minute for food is not the end of the world. In the end, the problems were handled in the most effective way possible to ensure that everyone's needs were met.

Essentially, when you are thinking critically, you are assessing, analyzing and acting. Each of these requires you to think effectively and ensure that you are rational, critical and open-minded, while making the decision that is appropriate for your current predicament. You will be able to do several thing like, showing an inclination to behave in ways that are inherently problem-solving oriented. On top of that, be intelligent and able to make rational/logical decisions. Effectively, you will be able to understand and interact with the world around you in a way that is deemed as thoughtful and functional.

Critical Thinking is:

Assessing:	Processing:	Applying
•You can see what is happening around you quickly	•You can comprehend what is happening around you and sort it into an order of most to least importance	•You can utilize your critical thinking skills to act in a way that is effective and conducive to solving the problem at hand

Types of Critical Thinking

Critical thinking is essential in our day to day life—you can use critical thinking when trying to solve a real life problem, such as the one discussed earlier. In a conversation your critical thinking skills can help to infer information that is not directly said but is heavily implied, such as someone giving several vague answers as to why they are hesitant to do something can be a way of saying No.

You may use it to disprove that click-bait article you scrolled past on social media that took a quote out of context and ran with it to make someone else look bad. Also when trying to figure out why a code that you have written is not functioning or what has died in your car by process of elimination.

In the process of thinking critically, you are trying to gain further information about something so as to make an informed decision. This usually involves going through several thought processes to arrive at that point. It can happen in various different ways. In fact, there are several different forms of critical thinking that are all related, and in some cases, overlapping in nature. They include:

- Anthropological or sociological thinking

- Historical thinking

- Legal thinking

- Logical thinking

- Mathematical thinking

- Musical thinking

- Political thinking

- Psychological thinking

- Philosophical or ethical thinking

- Scientific thinking

While looking over those forms, what stands out? Can you identify a way they may all be similar to each other? What do they have in common? If you can answer this, you are already using critical thinking skills— in that, you are using your background knowledge surrounding these subjects to find patterns, make inferences and apply that information.

In this case, what all of these have in common is that they look like they all belong in a college course listing—for a good reason. These are all considered academic fields. Academics tend to be heavily influenced by critical thinking, even when they may not seem like it. Art history, for example, has just as much critical thinking value as taking a class on philosophy or biology—you are still going to be gathering, interpreting and applying information to make informed and educated conclusions on the given data. Critical thinking skills determine your ability to be successful in an academic setting because academics themselves are so focused on learning, exploring and interpreting.

Most of the time, the first form of critical thinking that children become aware of, or at least the first one that comes to mind when cued to think about it, is the scientific method. The scientific method, basically comprises of six steps to follow in order to explore the world around you which is a never-ending cycle— first, you observe, hypothesize, test and gather results, analyze the results, and then either accept or reject the hypothesis that you have posited. In general, you are going to continue this cycle until you find an equilibrium between your hypothesis and your end results.

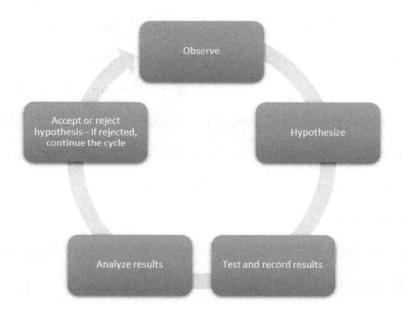

Why Critical Thinking Matters

These skills may seem abstract—after all, do you really need to be able to recite the scientific method or know what modus ponens is and how to use it in order to be effective in real-life scenarios? Some people may incorrectly assume that, just like teachers used to say that you need to learn how to do math by hand because you will not always have a calculator on hand, being able to use these critical thinking skills is something that is said to be needed but not actually relevant.

After all, when is the last time that you have used the equation to identify the area of a circle or needed the quadratic formula after you have graduated from high school or college?

Most people never use these skills again—if they are not directly relevant to their job, they will not need them. An artist may not need to know the area of a circle or how to make a perfect argument that is foolproof, so those critical thinking skills seem irrelevant. If an artist does not need to be thinking about abstract or concrete data, do they really need to be able to think critically?

The answer is yes—critical thinking is critical for a reason. These skills can be relevant in nearly any setting. You may not need to use math skills, but the skills behind those math skills, the fundamental critical thinking skills, are crucial and will be used again and again. You will use these skills in your relationships—such as when you need to make a compromise over something that you may feel quite passionate about but cannot get your partner to agree on. You may use them when trying to decide which car to get when your old one dies, or when trying to figure out which job makes the most sense to you. You will be able to create patterns and inferences based on smaller sums of information in ways that will be relevant to you in basic life.

Consider grocery shopping for a moment. You may go into the store with a concrete list in hand with a plan to get exactly what you came for and nothing else. As you look at your first item, it's tomato sauce, so you go to the canned aisle and look for the sauce. Suddenly, you realize that not only are there several different brands of sauce, but also different sizes of cans for the same brands. How do you know which one makes the most sense for you to buy? The smaller cans may look cheaper at a glance, but are they really? The larger cans cost more for the can, but if you look closely at the prices compared to what you get, you realize that—it saves to buy in bulk. The larger cans of tomato sauce are usually slightly cheaper per ounce.

To prove this, think about it this way: Your recipe calls for 24 oz. of tomato sauce. You can buy cans of 8 oz. of tomato sauce for $0.49 each, or you can buy cans of 16 oz. of tomato sauce for $0.85, or you can buy cans of 30 oz. of tomato sauce for $1.39 each. Now, let's add up the cost per oz. of each of these—this is quite simple. All you will need to do is divide the price of the can by the oz. within the can to get the price per oz.

When you do this, you find out that buying an 8 oz. can results in you effectively paying $0.0612/oz. while buying a 16 oz. can costs you $0.05312/oz., and buying a 30 oz. can of sauce will cost you $0.046333/oz.

With some critical thinking skills, you can now figure out that it makes more sense to buy the largest can of sauce, even if you are not going to use the whole thing. In order to buy the exact amount of sauce, you would have to buy three cans of the 8 oz. sauce, and you would spend $1.47. Even with you throwing away a small amount of sauce in buying a 30 oz. can, you are still only spending $1.39 for that can as opposed to $1.47 to get an exact amount with smaller numbers.

While a few cents may not seem like a big deal, this can add up exponentially. If you start to shop around and find cheaper ways to buy food, your food budget decreases, thanks to your ability to think critically. This is both meaningful and beneficial to you. Ultimately, everyone has to eat, and food always be an added cost unless you happen to be a serious homesteader able to produce everything you ever use at home. This means that critical thinking skills are relevant to you, even if you are not going to be working in a field that is largely technical, mathematical or scientific.

Chapter 2:

Core Critical Thinking Skills

Critical thinking is made up of several different skill sets that come together, allowing you to interpret and understand the information you are attempting to analyze. These skills are important in several different contexts, even if they may not necessarily seem important upfront. When you develop these skills, you become capable of managing nearly any situation that requires thinking and problem solving. The ability to make judgments that are both purposeful and reflective, allows you to handle anything that life throws your way.

Interpretation

The first important skills that you must master to think critically is interpretation. With this ability, you can comprehend and also communicate the significance of whatever it is that you are discussing. Consider that problem with your children again—they are all crying for help, and you need to figure out what to do with them. When you are able to interpret the situation, you gather information about what is around you and begin figuring out what is happening.

Meaning, you are able to recognize the significance of your experiences—therefore you can compare the children crying around you and their respective needs. The oldest child tends to only cry when there is something wrong, while the baby usually cries whenever anything is wrong, and so on. You are able to understand what is happening around you, thanks to your past experiences, situations, judgments, beliefs or other relevant instances.

There are other categories of sub-skills that are relevant: this sub- skills make you capable of truly understanding what you are interpreting. They include:

- **Categorization:** You can sort an event that you are currently observing into a category with similar past events. For example, times when your infant has cried for food.

- **Decoding significance:** You can figure out which events are significant versus insignificant or not worth attention. When your is child crying over the television that needs to be on, you are able to deem this inconsequential to everything else and choose to instead prioritize the child that is actively bleeding in front of you.

- **Clarifying meaning:** This entails being able to give a precise explanation for an outcome. For example—if someone walks into the room and sees everyone crying, you can tell that person exactly what is wrong with each child and the cause of their distress.

In other instances, each of these skills can be crucial in settings that are less real-life and more academic. Can you read through a news article and tell it's biased? That's interpretation— the ability to recognize that the news source you are reading must be biased toward a specific political alignment thanks to the wording, or through recognizing the author's name and knowing their own personal alignment.

Are you able to tell what someone is thinking by looking at their body language? This is interpreting their physical motions and actions into something more meaningful— when an individual storms at you angrily it's a show of aggressiveness, while someone who approaches you nervously is likely afraid of asking you for something. Each of these are ways in which interpretation is relevantly useful.

Analysis

The next important skill in critical thinking is analysis. This is the ability to identify the intended and actual relationships between what you are observing. These observations can be listening to what someone has said, observing actions, listening to a question and understanding its relevance. When you are able to analyze, you can understand the undertones of what is happening around you— by seeing the meaning behind actions rather than just seeing the actions as they are.

Like interpretation, analysis comprises of other sub-skills, such as:

- **Examining ideas:** You can look at something that is being presented to you and figure out what it's intended for. For example, when you see your child screaming and holding his bleeding head, and you can also see footprints on the desk, and a chair pushed over to it. Then you are able to connect the dots and figure out the relationship between the desk and the fact that the child is crying and bleeding—in fact, it's quite obvious that he climbed up, jumped and got hurt.

- **Detecting and decoding arguments:** When you can detect arguments, it's easy to understand what someone means when they talk you through something. You can see when they are supporting their points and simultaneously pointing out the weakness in your opinions. By listening to their arguments, you are able to respond logically and rationally, and voice any objections.

- **Analyzing any arguments that are decoded:** You can understand the meaning behind the argument that you have pieced together after listening to the other person's point of view—this means that you can understand what they are getting at, even if they are a bit vague. For example, if your child say, "Mama, I cleaned my room, I took care of all the toys and I made sure that my little sister had a toy to play with. Can I please have some tablet time?" From that argument you can easily tell that the child wants to be rewarded for his/ her efforts. Of course, most of the time, analyzing arguments will be a bit more complicated, but this childlike logic helps to get a solid understanding.

The ability to analyze what is being presented to you can be crucial in real-life instances. It means being able to weigh the pros and cons between two different choices to solve a problem, in other words—you can see an argument for both sides, analyze it and figure out which solution is superior.

Analyzing a newspaper can help in determining its purpose and whether it's worth reading. You can identify which claims are being made so as to figure out whether to support or criticize it—a crucial skill in adulthood, especially if you need to figure out a decision to make that has some serious implications.

Evaluation

The third skill necessary in critical thinking is evaluation. This is the ability to understand the credibility of an observation or information. First you take in the information presented to you, organize it and evaluate to determine whether your judgment is accurate or if the source is worth the time. You are able to understand and assess the validity and accuracy of an argument. That way you can choose to support or completely disregard it. As an adult this skill helps to figure out what is true or false, what has proper data backing it up or is worth ignoring or when something is entirely biased and not worth your time.

Evaluation doesn't comprise of any sub-skill, but it does have some incredibly important uses. With this ability you can identify how credible a speaker is or if this book is worth the time. You are able to understand this by looking at the representations of what is occurring around you or the relevance of the source you are evaluating: First, figure out if the description seems valid or if the opinion and belief are backed up accordingly. Secondly, figure out if what is being said seems legitimate or if it's making up statistics in an attempt to sway your beliefs to the opposite direction.

In being able to judge the credibility, you can differentiate between typical forwarding email chains claiming that you will find $100,000 in one week if you forward the email to 10 other people versus a letter from an attorney informing you that your long awaited settlement offer is $100,000. By evaluating how each email is presented you are able to make a valid and informed decision on whether it's credible or not. Was the email sent by your attorney, whom you have recently been in contact with, probably waiting for a settlement, or was it from a random personal email address you have never heard before? Was the email riddled with spelling mistakes, chat speak and typos, or was it professional and encrypted to ensure that the email is harder to crack? Looking at all this and making sound judgement will protect you from being scammed or having your personal information stolen and used against you later on.

Inference

Next, it is important to learn about inference—this skill is crucial for further critical thinking beyond the first three skills. When you can infer, you are able to accurately identify or get the necessary information needed to make a reasonable conclusion. It is the ability to create thought out and intelligent hypotheses based on relevant and trustworthy information. On top of that, it is the ability to consider the consequences based on the data at hand—you can figure out what will come next based on the information that you have already gleaned. This is essentially the step of making a hypothesis that you may have been taught in elementary or middle school science class.

Inference comprises of subskills, such as:

- **Querying evidence:** This allows you to question the evidence at hand and gather further and relevant details needed to make a valid decision and interpretation of a study.

- **Conjecturing alternatives:** Ability to consider other possible outcomes other than the expected. In other words, it's recognizing that sometimes, things will not play out exactly as you hope. For example, if you are going to throw a rock at something, you may expect the target will break, but it could also scratch, dent, or be completely undamaged. You can weigh the likelihood of each of those inferences based on your understanding of everything at hand.

- **Drawing conclusions:** You can look at everything that has been presented to you and arrive at a logical conclusion. In building upon all of the previous skills, you will identify the conclusion that makes the most sense and determine that it ought to be the most likely outcome, then defend it with the information that you have.

As you can see, this particular skill can be incredibly valuable in understanding the world around you. Both as a hard skill in a science field where you are actively carrying out experiments, but also in relationships and interpersonal interactions whereby you are able to weigh the outcome of an action that you have chosen to perform. For example, if you are fighting with your spouse because you both strongly feel that the other is wrong, you can infer the best way to resolve the situation—if you are able to end the argument by gifting your wife her favorite food and flowers after work and apologizing. Inferring that this situation will be no different, and doing exactly that might end the argument.

Explanation

It is nearly impossible to truly have a solid understanding of how something works if you cannot explain it, and that is what makes the explanation portion of critical thinking so important—when you are able to explain yourself well, you can explain coherently exactly why you have done something and how it seemed like the best possible solution. You can allow the other person to effectively see things through your eyes when you have the verbal know-how and technical understanding necessary to walk the other person through your decision. Explanation allows you communicate and justify the reasoning that was involved in making your decision, as well as to present that reasoning in a coherent manner that is clear to understand.

It comprises of sub-skills, such as:

- **Describing your method and results:** You are able to explain your actions in a way that is easily understood by those around you so they can see things from your perspective. For example, you explain why you thought buying the ground beef with a slightly higher fat content seemed okay to you in the absence of the type that you were asked to bring because it was so similar.

- **Justifying what you have done:** You can explain exactly why the decisions you made were right—this is through walking the other person through your explanation for them to understand why you considered those decisions right. You can point out why you didn't to buy a certain extra insurance coverage for your car because you did not see it as worthwhile when the car is falling apart due to age, so why pay for extra coverage that would likely never be put in use?

- **Proposing and defending your explanation clearly:** This entails bring up support for exactly why you made your decision in a way that makes sense. You can tell your child

29

that you are not willing to get them a puppy for Christmas because they can't keep their room clean or complete chores without constant supervision, in that case, you feel like adding a puppy is too much of a responsibility.

- **Presenting well-reasoned arguments in context:** This involves outlining reasons for making a choice in a logical and sensible way. First, bring up any supporting evidence, then explain the contexts of that evidence, finally apply that evidence to your argument in a way that makes sense. For example, if you point out all the ways that your child is not responsible before telling them that a dog takes responsibility and only responsible children get puppies. The logical conclusion is that your child does not get a puppy because they are not responsible enough.

This skill, in particular, is incredibly useful in activities that require extensive attention to detail, logic and practical reasoning. This helps in figuring out whether an argument is rational. Additionally, lawyers can use this when defending a client. It can be used to better interpersonal communication therefore allowing you to easily clear up any negative implications or misunderstandings.

Self-Regulation

The final skill that is crucial to critical thinking is self-regulation. This skill is the ability to self-consciously monitor your own thought processes and behaviors. It is about how you are using those thoughts and actions in order to get results, allowing for a confirmation or a rejection of one's inferential judgments. It allows you to question, confirm, justify or correct your reasoning skills used in earlier steps of the process.

Self-regulation comprises of two sub-skills, that is:

- **Self-examination:** This means being willing to look at yourself and figure out if you are on the right track or if your views are controversial or even wrong. You are able to admit if there are any self-bias or other negative implications on your reasoning that are making it difficult for your judgment to be considered rational or sound.

- **Self-correction:** You are able to make any corrections for issues discovered during your self-examination. Once you find that you're your choice is wrong, you are willing to go through the process to fix it so you can make sure it aligns with the right choice to begin with rather than trying to push harder and try to make sure that your mistakes are somehow justified, even when they should not be.

Overall, when you master the art of self-regulation, you are able to always accurately self-evaluate. It gives you the ability to make right decisions than selfish ones, it makes sure you fight the urge to make unethical, illegal and logically inconsistent decisions no matter how convenient they may be. Finally if you have made a mistake, you seek to make it right— for example, if something you said offends someone, you are willing to learn, understand why what you said was offensive, and correct from it in the future.

Chapter 3:

A Portrait of the Critical and Not-So-Critical Thinkers

Strong critical thinkers are more effective in life. They are able to approach situations in ways that make more sense and are able to be defended logically. They are less prone to being caught into behaving in ways that are impulsive or incorrect, and because of that, it is imperative that you learn to be a critical thinker. For a critical thinker, life is easier—it is everywhere in life. The ability to think critically is necessary in so many situations around you, from how likely you are to succeed in a job that is quite technical and mathematical to the likelihood of having a happy and successful relationship. Let's look at some of the most notable traits of both a critical and not-so-critical individual to see the real difference between them.

The Critical Thinker's Portrait

When you develop your ability to think critically, you will notice a boost in all sorts of characteristics that make you more socially desirable. You will become someone that more people want to be around and more emotionally intelligent—one of those buzzwords in today's society for the ability to get along well with others and effectively manage relationships and interactions with others, thanks to being able to understand and control yourself and your own emotional states. This is all due to a culmination of several other traits, such as:

Inquisitive

Critical thinkers are inquisitive—they are constantly willing to ask questions and understand the world around them. They are driven by their desire to understand others better and will make it a point to learn about different topics and how they impact others.

Attentive to Times Where Critical Thinking Is Necessary

The critical thinker is well-aware of the strength of his or her abilities and is constantly on the lookout for situations in which critical thinking is necessary and warranted. Whenever it feels like critical thinking could be relevant, it is used, even if there may be an easier and simpler solution.

Self-Confidence

A critical thinker is confident that he or she is able to reason at any given time or situation and come up with a solution.

Open-Mindedness

A critical thinker is willing to recognize that world viewpoints are different, and that is okay—they are willing to entertain other opinions and assertions, giving them the same benefit of the doubt that they would give to others.

Flexibility

Critical thinker understand the need for flexibility especially when considering opposing viewpoints. They are willing to think about those difficult issues with the attention they deserve and will not shut down when presented with a viewpoint that does not align with theirs, and they are able to roll with the flow when something goes wrong and needs to be changed accordingly.

Alertness

Critical thinkers can anticipate and prepare for future outcomes by being aware of what happens around them.

Understanding Other People's Opinions

For a critical thinker other people's views are crucial, therefore they will listen to what other people think, even if they disagree with those beliefs, or they feel like they are irrelevant or unimportant. They will make it a point to listen and understand the other person's opinion rather than immediately dismiss it as illegitimate.

Fair in Appraising Reasoning

A critical thinker will not judge other people's approaches unfairly—they will make it a point to give every argument a fair judgment. Therefore, an argument will not be dismissed for not aligning with their personal opinions.

Honest

Critical thinkers are able to understand their own biases and prejudices, accept and fix them accordingly. This is the ability to self-control and self-regulate.

Understanding When to Stop, Make and Alter Judgments

Understanding when it is appropriate to stop making judgement or change it, based on feedback and understanding of the situation is a crucial trait for a critical thinker.

Willingness to Reconsider and Revisit Viewpoints When Change Is Necessary

A critical thinker can tell when it's fit to reconsider their opinion if at all it laced with negativity and it's invalid.

The Not-So-Critical Thinker's Portrait

A non- critical thinker is someone who's unable to manage thinking critically on a regular basis. This results to having a biased and judgmental individual, someone who can't accept other people's judgement and opinions. Such people struggle in their relationships and careers, since it's impossible to find a job that doesn't require some sort of higher-level thinking skills. Below are some common characteristics of the non-critical thinker.

Pretentious and Unable to Accurately Self-Analyze

A non-critical thinker is a people pleaser —they may say that they know or understand something out of embarrassment rather than admit the truth. Most of the time, they are unaware of their own weaknesses or limitations.

Think of Conflict as a Threat to the Ego or an Annoyance

Someone struggling to think critically is likely to see any sort of conflict that may arise as a threat to the ego rather than something that requires attention. If anyone tries to refute them, they feel threatened or annoyed and dismiss the claims without reflection.

Impatient and Unwilling to Learn

A non- critical thinker tends to be impatient—if something is complex, they will skip to the end with a best guess rather than attempting to really understand it. They would rather rush through to the end instead of learning, even though this means that they are still left in confusion.

Follow Gut Reactions Instead of Evidence

The non-critical thinker is more focused on feelings and gut reactions. For instance, if they are told to decide between a sports car and SUV, they will opt for the sports car because it makes them excited, even though the SUV is more useful. They are so caught up in their feelings that they do not pay attention to data and evidence, and this can cause them to behave impulsively instead of logically.

Preoccupied with Themselves

This type of thinkers are preoccupied with their own opinions of the world, and because of that, they are unwilling to entertain anyone else's viewpoint.

As soon as someone voices that they disagree, the non-critical thinker starts focusing on how best to refute the claim rather than making it a point to learn the other person's viewpoint, which may be quite valid. The preference will always be given to viewpoints that are in agreement with them or in viewpoints that are supportive of their own.

Chapter 4:

Benefits of Critical Thinking

Critical thinking is consciously and unconsciously around us, therefore it's quite useful. It' only beneficial to those who practice it effectively, and if you are willing and able to learn how to think critically, you too, can reap those benefits.

There are six key benefits of critical thinking that will be particularly discussed in this book. They include: becoming successful at work, being a better decision-maker, leading a happier life, ensuring you keep well-formed opinions, having better relationship and being a more informed citizen and member of society in general. While these benefits may sound technical and vague, they are attainable once one commits themselves to becoming a critical thinker. Let's take a closer look at each of them.

Successful Career

There are many instances in which critical thinking is crucial for a career. Which careers absolutely require it in order for you to be successful? Your list might comprise of—lawyers, analysts, doctors, scientists, and other people in careers that are technical and based upon science. While those people absolutely use critical thinking skills in their daily work responsibilities, what about jobs that people generally consider low-stakes?

It's easily assumed that some jobs are for uneducated and unintelligent individuals, for example waitressing and working at a fast-food joint, on the contrary this jobs also require critical thinking. Because without this skill, you can't decide which food should be cooked first in a customer's order. Also when figuring out whether to bring someone their drinks before they order or where to set a table for someone with a wheelchair, an infant in a car seat or someone who will otherwise take up a large area in the walkway right next to the kitchen. Poor customer like, constantly serving cold fries because you prioritized making the fries first since they are the easiest without considering the time the fries will sit as you assemble the rest of the order, may result to several complaints, and if they pile up might be fired.

Critical thinking is relevant in any career path. Since you will need to think, solve problems or help other people. In fact, it is actually becoming an incredibly desired skill as our society, at least in the United States, shifts into the fourth industrial revolution. With computers and machines that are able to perform menial tasks, the need for menial, low-intelligence necessary jobs, such as flipping burgers, or even taking orders, is less. The jobs that are largely considered to be beginner jobs are less common. Walking into your local fast-food restaurant lately, you may see options advertising mobile or kiosk ordering in which you never have to speak to a person to place an order. This means that jobs that require low skills become less in demand, and the jobs that are available become dependent on critical thinking.

Critical thinking itself is considered a soft skill—an important attribute that is recognized as being required to succeed at work. This is usually listed alongside emotional intelligence, creativity and other skills that are not necessarily written into the job description, but are implied and necessary to really function effectively. As a critical thinker, you are more legible and able to perform better because of the ability to solve problems with ease.

Better Decision Maker

Think for a moment the last time you made a decision. Not necessarily an important one. What about the decision before, and the decision before that? If you think about it, you are making decisions countless times throughout the day—you decide which shoes to wear based on the weather, whether to take the short or long way to work depending upon time and whether to stop for coffee, or even what to drink when you open the refrigerator. Some decisions that you make are quite menial and unimportant, and mostly unconscious. But what about the bigger decisions that you may be pressed to make?

These decisions are more impactful, such as whether to marry your partner, when to have children, buy a new house or move to a new town or city where you might be happier. Such decisions determine a major part of your life, and they can be difficult to make. However, when you are able to think critically, you can make better decisions. You are able to weigh the pros and cons to avoid making irrational or bad decision.

This is also relevant in other life aspects—which car to buy? Will you take advantage of that deal being advertising, which may or may not be so good? Whether to call out someone for lying. As a critical thinker, you will weigh the situation, accurately analyzing and evaluating it, before deciding.

Happier Life

The vast majority of people in the world strive for happiness in one form or another. They want to live their best life. However, that quality of life can be difficult to ascertain if you do not know what you are doing or you cannot make good decisions.

Using the critical thinking skill you can identify any cognitive biases and negative thought processes that impact your life negatively and break free from. Additionally, you can accurately assess your strengths and weaknesses, which boost makes you more confident. This skill can make you happier in general, as the self-confident individual is happier.

Happiness maybe an afterthought to the others, but it is incredibly important. It improves your quality of life, relationships and ability to communicate. In the end, one is fulfilled in life.

Well-Formed Opinions

When you were a child, did your teacher insist on the need to learn how to use an encyclopedia (the book, not online!) and make sure that you could do math by hand? Usually, they would always emphasize that you would not always have access to the internet or a calculator—but the joke is on them. The majority of people now hold the entirety of human knowledge in their back pocket or purse at almost all times thanks to the invention of smartphones. While these certainly do have their own limitations, such as being somewhere without reception. Regardless, people have access to nearly everything with a few presses of buttons on screens.

However, this has its own limitations. Information is everywhere, but not everything on the internet or Wikipedia is legitimate. This is where critical thinking skills come in. You need to be able to read and understand which of your sources are valid versus invalid. Think of the people who after two hours on Google are suddenly convinced that vaccinations are a conspiracy rather than something to protect people from getting sick and dying from horrible illnesses— this is a clinical example of lack critical thinking skills. Meaning, they don't analyze the credibility of their source of information. As a critical thinker, your opinions will be well informed and backed by legitimate sources rather than clickbait and controversy.

Better Relationships

Critical thinking does not mean that you must be robotic and harshly logical at all times—those people are rarely successful in their relationships and interactions with others, largely because they are so focused on cold, hard logic that they forget that people are not wholly logical. Just because humans can think logically does not mean that emotions are. In fact, rationality and emotionality may as well be opposites—they are so far from each other, thanks to their natures. Rationality originates from the brain, while emotionality is from the heart.

However, when you are a critical thinker, you are not a cold thinker—you are able to identify different viewpoints, relate and understand them better. You are empathetic and able to recognize that people can differ in some ways. While also accepting those differences and recognizing the value that they can bring to you. Critical thinking does not take your ability to empathize away—it tops up the ability to stay calm and in control during arguments. It allows you to see the situation at hand clearly, even when emotions are involved. Additionally, allowing you to avoid being manipulated and lied to.

Being an Informed Citizen

Perhaps one of the most important benefits, is your ability to be informed. Being able to deal with arising issues and find solutions by seeing it from all angles.

A critical thinker is not likely to fall victim to any form of manipulation or scare tactics. Instead, they point out fake news or when the attempts to rationalize something are inconsistent.

Finally, being able to make rational judgements, in ways that are logically consistent.

Chapter 5:

Obstacles to Critical Thinking and How to Overcome Them

Critical thinking, sounds quite easy on paper but it's not always achievable. Despite detailed everything has been laid out for you. It is a skill that can be difficult to develop if you are not in the right mindset or if you have any reservations that hold you back. In order to become a critical thinker, it is crucial to overcome any obstacles that night be standing in the way. Some of the common obstacles include:

Trusting the Gut

A common phrase in books, movies and even in several self-help books is "trust your gut". This is usually used when you are in doubt—if you are unsure whether you want to get a new job or work harder in your current one, many people may tell you vaguely to trust your gut because only you can make that decision. However, giving your gut too much power can begin to override your ability to think critically. Considering that your gut reaction is often your emotional reaction rather than the intellectual and rational reaction, at times this can be misleading since it affects the ability to see the world logically.

Trusting your gut is relying on intuition, something that has, in the past, been defined as the absence of analysis, meaning that it is automatic. This also means that it is emotional. It's a very thin line between being automatic and emotional, it is difficult to turn off your intuition, no matter how much you may wish that you could. Sometimes it's easier to listen to it rather than allowing yourself to think rationally about the situation. Instead of problem-solving when someone tells you that they do not have the product that you had hoped to buy, you may get angry and refuse to buy anything at all. Is losing that product that big of a deal? Probably not. However, it can be difficult to overcome that immediate emotional impulse known as intuition.

This can be problematic because any of those rational decisions that would ordinarily filter out problems biases are turned off to allow for intuition to rule, there are usually large errors that come out in hindsight. You may have responded emotionally to one instance, only to realize after the fact that your attempt to bypass rationality was actually quite wrong, and now you are in a situation that is much worse. For example, imagine that your car dies. Instead of stopping to have it looked at, you declare that your car is unreliable and dive into a $30,000 debt to get a new one instead. A week later, someone asks you if you had ever tested the battery on your car—at that point, you realize that you made a grave mistake that instead of looking into other options, you were swayed by emotion and decided to buy a new car instead of trying to fix the old one.

There are several ways that you can get around this trust your gut mentality. The two most beneficial ones being never make a decision immediately and to always stop and speculate on the possibility that things are actually fine and could be fixed in a way that is not necessarily the intuitive. However, there are very few decisions that must be made immediately. When you are making decisions that are particularly hefty or weighty, you need to take the time to think about it logically devoid of emotional influence. It can be easy to be caught up in the concern that your current car is entirely unreliable after it has died, but if you have not had it evaluated by a mechanic, there is no way to know. Instead of rushing to the dealership to take out a loan, you should try sleeping on the decision instead. You are in no rush to determine what the right course of action is so resist being pressured by time limits. In taking the time to let the emotions pass, you will be able to have a clearer image of what is going on.

Fearing Failure

Sometimes, what scares you the most when you are making decisions, and inhibits your ability to think rationally and critically, is a fear of failure. When you are convinced that you might fail, it is difficult to overcome those reservations. It can be crippling to think that you are going to make the wrong decision, even when you have severally gone through all the possible outcomes. You are therefore afraid of making the wrong decision, the most comfortable option being doing nothing at all.

It is tough to deny that fear in the back of your mind, but accommodating cripples the ability to think critically. Since you are worrying about whether you are making the right decision or not. Some of the problems resulting from fear of failure include:

- **Hesitation:** You are reluctant to try new things or projects that may challenge you or possibly be outside of your ability range

- **Self-sabotage:** When you are afraid, you may procrastinate, fail and miss out on great opportunities simply because fear made you feel inadequate.

- **Low self-esteem**: When you struggle with your self-esteem, you may not even bother trying to make a decision in the first place—you may feel like it does not matter what you do since you will fail anyway, so you do not think critically about the situation at hand

- **Perfectionism**: When you struggle with a fear of failure, you might become obsessed with the need to always want more, which can be really draining. When critical thinking itself is a process in which you are eliminating situations that did not quite play out as planned, you are essentially failing over and over again to arrive at the right conclusion. This is difficult when you are perfectionistic.

Interestingly, even though the fear of failure is a massive barrier between you and critical thinking, it is through critical thinking that you are able to defeat it. It is one of those situations in which you have to push past it in order to see that failure is not as bad as you originally thought, though you might fail, there are solutions to fix it. Critical thinking itself involves several skills that can help assuage that fear such as: an analysis of possible outcomes, an elimination of negative, biased or generally unhelpful perceptions and creating contingency plans in case your attempts to think critically failed the first time around.

Fearing the Backlash

Sometimes, what is holding you back from thinking critically is fearing the backlash that will come with making the decision you are leaning toward making. You might have the best rational decision, but while enforcing it, you will face some sort of backlash. Perhaps the backlash will come from those around you hating the decision. For instance deciding to ban cell phones at the workplace so as to up productivity. You know that banning cell phones will help, but this decision will be met with all sorts of backlash because naturally, people hate being ordered around.

This fear of backlash can lead to a clog in your critical thinking. While you are so caught up in wanting to please everyone making unbiased decisions is an uphill task. If you were thinking critically, the concern about the backlash would have been irrelevant. You would have acknowledged that your colleagues wouldn't be pleased but what mattered was the right decision.

In order to revive the art critical thinking, first get over the backlash and accept it as part of the process. This is by making the conscious decision to no longer allow that fear to rule. Although it's easier said than done, with practice and perseverance you can overcome.

Once you let go of the opinions of others and other biases then will you be able to see things rationally. It can be difficult at first, but try writing a pros and cons sheet of why you should and should not enact the policy or decision you are debating. Next thing is eliminating all the choices that might be strongly influenced by emotions rather than reason. By doing so, the decision will be well thought out and made with a clear mind.

Think of the surgeon, in the operating room, who suddenly realizes they made a mistake and need to think fast. Making a decision that may paralyze or cripple a patient or the alternative which is doing nothing and a life is lost. In instances like that, tough choices must be made without fear of backlash—they need to have the wherewithal to make the decision clearly and quickly without thinking about the emotions of the people waiting outside for the patient.

Struggling to Cope with Change

Fearing change can be an obstacle that hinders critical thinking. You may be struggling to admit that you are wrong or maybe feeling like making a change will be too extreme and the alternative is more comfortable. A non-critical is more likely to feel threatened by change and failing to admit when they are wrong. After all, if you cannot admit that your own opinion or perception is faulty, how can you possibly claim to be thinking rationally?

To really understand this, think of the following argument: If I like pizza, the sky is green. I do like pizza, therefore the sky is green. Is this logically valid? Yes—it follows a readily accepted form of argument. However, does it make sense? Anyone who is a critical thinker can look outside right now and say with certainty that the sky is not, in fact, green.

This means that the argument is not sound. However, if you struggle to cope with change and have grown up saying that exact argument, despite the fact that everyone around you is pointing up at the sky and telling you that it is clearly blue, not green, so why will you refuse to see otherwise, you may dig in your heels and exclaim, "But I like pizza! If I like pizza, then the sky is blue!" Yes, your argument is technically still valid. However, your failure to cope when you are presented with evidence that directly refutes it means that you cannot think critically.

Being a critical thinker does not necessarily imply you will always be right. Therefore, it's crucial to be able to deal with being incorrect and having a flawed idea. First step is admitting for low-stakes occurrences, such as if you accidentally cut someone off in a queue in the coffee shop or if you dropped something and it got ruined. Instead of getting defensive and feigning innocence, admit that you were wrong. Roll with the change.

Chapter 6:

Preparing to Become a Critical

Thinker

While you can prepare yourself emotionally to be a critical thinker, or make sure that you are going through the right motions, sometimes, it helps to make sure your body is prepared as well. Remember, your body and mind are intricately linked—your body is your mind's vessel to work and thrive, so if you want to have the mental capacity and energy to really allow your mind to embrace critical thinking, you need to make sure you are taking care of it well.

This chapter will provide you with four distinct tips to ensure that you are, ultimately able to think critically by taking care of your body. You will be priming your mind to think clearly and effectively by making sure you follow these general health guidelines. The step are basic and doable, for instance, using moderate levels of caffeine, cutting out refined sugars and avoiding over-eating. Doing this is a step in the right direction toward priming the body and mind to think critically.

Moderate Caffeine Use

- Moderate levels of caffeine act as a stimulant that increases awareness and responsiveness

Cut Refined Sugars

- Refined sugars keep your body and mind from functioning at their best

Avoid Overeating

- Eat enough to live healthily-- do not live to eat

Diet and the Mind

It is well-known that there is a connection between your diet and mental health. If you want to ace a test, eating enough food will nourish your mind and boost functionality. Think of a toy remote control car—with old batteries it will move slowly or not at all.

However, with new batteries, it will be at its optimum performance. Instead of lagging and struggling to respond, it will function as intended.

A similar occurrence happens with your mind—when you give it the proper nourishment that it needs, it will function to its fullest extent. Your brain uses a significant amount of energy, considering how small it is compared to the rest of your body— the brain uses about 300 calories a day in order to function. This means that you need to keep it well-nourished if you want it to work well, with the right amount of nutrients.

Moderate Caffeine Use

Caffeine is a drug, readily available in most products. It is in coffee, tea, sodas and more. Most people generally overlook its usage, despite the fact that it has several important benefits to the body. In fact, caffeine, when consumed in moderate amounts, can actually improve your thinking capabilities, which is an advantage for a critical thinker.

When you consume caffeine, it is quickly and readily absorbed into the body system—it only takes between 15 and 40 minutes for caffeine to reach peak levels in the bloodstream. Once there, it works by blocking adenosine, a neurotransmitter used by your brain. In inhibiting the levels of adenosine, then the dopamine, norepinephrine, and glutamate levels go up. This means that the individual that has consumed the caffeine is less tired and instead feels better, more effective and energized. It has been shown to have a positive effect on attention and cognitive performance, thanks to its effect on alertness and arousal. Caffeine is, overall, quite effective as a stimulant without compromising any function or mental acuity elsewhere.

In consuming caffeine, you are boosting alertness, by lowering error rates in reaction time tasks and increasing visual vigilance. It enables you to pay attention over a longer period of time, with that attention being deemed as more efficient in general. What does this mean for your critical thinking skills, then?

They go up. Because you can focus longer, think quicker without feeling sleepy or groggy. In other words, you are able to do critical thinking tasks quicker and clearer than you would have been able to otherwise. So you should totally have that afternoon cup of coffee if you are going to be in meetings all day or otherwise busy with tasks that require attention to detail. Note: a moderate dose of caffeine is between 200-300 mg.

Cut out the Sugar

Sugar is quite bad for your health—particularly the refined type that is found in most of today's food and beverages. Especially with nearly every type of food coming in a low fat or fat-free option, it is easy to go well over the daily recommended dose of sugar. When you eliminate fat from a product, some of the flavor is removed, and to make up for it, sugar is added in.

However, studies show that sugar is not good for the brain. It has been shown that sugar can make you grumpy, tired or prone to make bad decisions. The best way to avoid this negative impacts is by cutting it out altogether. Of course, this is far easier said than done—if you take a look at the nutrition levels on some of your food, especially the processed or convenience food, chances are that you are eating far more than your recommended daily allotment, even they are not sweet foods. Some of the foods containing refined sugars include: white bread, pasta yogurts sugared coffee and processed juice.

When you cut these out of your diet, you will have less food choices. Did you know that the spaghetti sauce that you buy premade at the store is full of added sugar? What about mayonnaise? Ketchup? All of it is usually laden with sugar or high-fructose corn syrup, which is another fancy word for refined sugar from a different source.

However, you can always eat natural sugar, such as sugar in fruits and vegetables. This is a safe option compared to the refined sugar. Cutting processed sugar has incredible results on the body. Such as, clearing brain fog, ability to think and feel and be conscious of ones surroundings. Of course, this comes with time—the first few days, you will crave sugar since it's an addiction. Nevertheless, if you are able to stick to the guns and make sure you cut it out for good, the end result is a well-nourished, healthy brain. After the first week and a half to two weeks, you will find that you feel more clear-headed and focused. The bottom line is, cutting sugar is a form of self-care that cannot be underestimated.

Avoiding Overeating

Studies show that, even though you may have all sorts of healthy food at your disposal, eating it in excess can greatly impair cognitive function. Overeating and giving the brain too much caloric intake can actually increase the chances of suffering from memory loss or mild cognitive impairment.

Therefore, it's important to understand the correlation between how much you eat and your brain functionality. Only eat when you are hungry not as a way of killing boredom and make sure that the food you eat is healthy and nourishing. Your body and mind will both thank you.

Overeating can have negative impacts on someone's wellbeing. In that, it may make one experience mood swings and depression. Both of those problems can directly impact your ability to think clearly and effectively. If you struggle with overeating, or you are not aware of how much food you eat, consider use of a food tracker—this way you can count the calories on an app on your phone and stay within your recommended limit of the day.

In so doing, the body and the mind will be able to function better.

Chapter 7:

The Critical Thinking Process

Thinking critically does not have to be as difficult as it may seem. While it may be intimidating to have all of this information that has been provided, you can use it to your advantage as you master it. As with most other skills, it's important to put in the effort of practicing and honing these skills until they are well-developed. When you do this, you are able to really understand the world around you. Considering your own thought, you become aware of several of these processes occurring, though many of them may also be automatic in decisions that are simple and straight-forward.

The process of critical thinking includes the following steps: gathering knowledge, comprehending the knowledge, applying the knowledge, analyzing the application, a synthesis of the analysis and information learned and gathered, finally, the action taken. At the end of the process, you then identify whether your application was actually accurate, and if it is not, then you may need to revisit the beginning of the process, looking for new inferences that can be made.

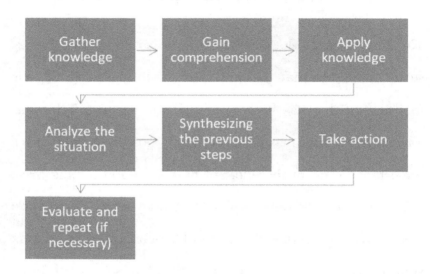

Gather Knowledge

At the beginning of each and every attempt to think critically is the gathering of knowledge. This can be as simple as identifying the problem at hand. Think back to the situation at the beginning of the book—you are faced with four children that are crying for attention, and you need to figure out who to help first and how to help each child in a way that calms their distress as fast as possible.

However, not all situations are as simple. Some situations require higher level of thinking to find to get a right solution. Therefore, this step should be instead reserved for figuring out what the problem is in the first place.

During this stage, you will be asking questions in order to gain that deep understanding of the problem, if there is one. If there is no problem and you are instead analyzing something that has been presented to you, you can move on to the next step. If not, you should work on exploring the issues. Overall, this step can be summarized with the following two questions:

What is wrong or the problem?

Why does this problem need to be solved?

Comprehension

When you know what the problem is, you now can begin to understand the situation altogether. At this point, you may ask yourself why the children are crying in the first place—it is time to start gathering up as much data as you possibly can, to get a solid understanding of the situation. You use this stage to gather relevant data that can help solve the problem. This is primarily the stage in which you collect data with any research methods necessary—this could be through simple observation, researching the problems, choosing to outsource to an expert that will provide more sophisticated insight or any other option that will allow you to gather an understanding of the situation.

At this stage, you are focused on *gathering information that will be necessary to understand the problem.*

Remember, knowledge is power. While you might gather a lot of information, you are not actually obligated to use every piece of data. For example, imagine looking around trying to figure out why everyone is crying. There's blood on the eldest, at the same time that the youngest eats, then the middle child is crying while covering their ears and the other, desperately waving around a remote in the air to get help. Also there's the stench from the baby who need a diaper change, and the desk chair that has been moved to assist in climbing. You can see footprints on the desk, a toy bat on the floor next to the oldest child as well, which conceivably could have been wielded by one of the other children to hit him over the head, causing the bleeding. At this stage, you gather all of the evidence in the room to understand the problem. You are not yet concerned with analyzing it, but rather just identifying it.

Application

The third step of this process is known as application. At this stage, you are focusing further on the information that was gathered in the previous step. It involves application, understanding the different resources and building a link between the information at hand and the resources you have gathered. Think of this as the recognition and application of the information to the problem that you have.

At this point, you are closely looking at the information you gathered and beginning to assign it to what you see. If the child is bleeding—that was probably due to jumping off of the desk, judging by the footprints, or due to the bat being swung at him. The discomfort of the diaper is the obvious reason the baby is crying. For the child covering her ears and crying, the logical assumption is that her ears hurt and she is feeling overwhelmed. Lastly, the child waving the remote around clearly wants to watch television because the show has stopped auto streaming. You are beginning to connect data to problems.

Of course, in situations that require more mental power, you may require to create a mental map to link the relationship between the situation and the problem you are trying to solve.

Creating a mind map involves writing down the problem at hand in the center of a piece of paper. This may be something, such as "NEED MONEY" or any other problem that you may be facing. From there, write out three different related possible solutions or tangents of the problem. Perhaps you write down around needing money that you could apply for jobs, sell off some unused goods, take out a loan, borrow money from a friend or do an odd job that you find in your local classifieds ad.

Now, you have several different tangents surrounding the situation at hand that could be possible solutions to your problem. Off of each of those tangents, you would then branch out what was necessary surrounding them. For example, you may write down around applying for jobs that you could look online, search in person and update your resume to reflect the correct information. Lastly, continue with this process around each and every step until you no longer need to flesh out your plans to tell the way forward.

This kind of procedure may look disorganized to someone who does not necessarily know what your thought processes involved. Regardless, you have related the gathered information whether through research or by figuring out the problem through brainstorming, and it is all related to the problem and ready to be addressed in the next step.

Analysis

The next step necessary in the critical thinking process is analysis. During this stage, everything is put on the table including the mental map written out with all of the data, or not if the problem wasn't complex. At this point, you are identifying the strong and weak points, and figuring out the challenges to the situation and solutions to arising challenges. At this stage, you are going to be applying everything and analyzing it. During this stage, you may also weigh the pros and cons of each of the possible solutions.

If the problem does not need nearly as much attention, you may just make snap analyses, such as when you determine that your child was hurt while jumping off the desk. This happens more automatic because the evidence is obvious. However, identifying this as the cause of his bleeding and crying is still the application of critical thinking skills.

Synthesis

Once you are done analyzing the problem at hand, it's time to come up with an action plan. At this point, you know what has happened, got your background and necessary information to help in making a proper verdict of the situation. This means that the gathered information is organized. If you are trying to figure out the best way to get money, first priority would be putting belongings you don't use up for sale. This will cover the current financial needs while you work on securing a job for the long term financial needs.

When trying to figure out how to stop everyone from crying, this is where you start to rank the order of importance— recognize that head injuries are no joke and choose to address that first, followed by the diaper which could cause a diaper rash, then turning on the television, and finally feeding the baby. You make the plan in your mind, so you know how best to tackle the problem.

For issues that will require more strenuous thinking, you may find that writing out the steps to the plan will be beneficial. This steps will be a guide, so you do not get lost along the way. In doing so, you will easily get through the process, even when it may be stressful.

You may feel like you are getting frazzled with all of the screaming around you, so you repeat the order to yourself as you go through everything: "Head, diaper, television, food and silence." For something more difficult, you will follow step-by-step guide as you go through the process.

Taking Action

Finally, the last step where you will actively implement the plan that you have set in motion. You are going through the process of solving the problem in the way that you chose to pursue, recognizing that the method you have chosen is the best in your particular situation. You would then follow the plan of action that you have created in the previous step.

When taking action, try to keep it consistent, unless some other information arises. Meaning, it's essential to consider any additional feedback that is relevant to the situation or will directly impact your capability to move towards the intended direction. After all, critical thinking encourages you to become flexible and to think as rational as possible. If rationally, you have gathered enough information halfway through your action plan that contradicts the initial approach you had taken, then you should absolutely stop and approach it from a different angle.

For example, if trying to pursue short-term loans first is not in your best interest after a past bad experience, you may instead opt to look for gigs online. However, if someone suggests that donating plasma can get you paid, you may choose to do that instead, even though it was not on your list. Just because you have made a plan at this point in time does not mean you are bound to it by law—changing it is well within your rights if you consider it necessary.

Evaluation

After you are done executing your plan, it is time to evaluate it for effectiveness. While sometimes, this is quite straightforward, like knowing that you were successful when the children are calm and silent. Other times, it requires you to actually dig and ensure that the problem is in fact fixed. You may need further testing, for example, to confirm that the problem is no longer a problem. You may need to have someone look over the conclusion to ensure that it is accurate. Also, you may submit the work and then assume that it will be evaluated before you find out if you did it right.

If you realize that you have failed at any point in time, then it is time to start at the beginning—figure out why the cause of the failure and then eliminate your current solution from your list of possibilities. Learn from the failure where possible but don't feel beat up or defeated. You have eliminated a possible solution from your list, and that alone teaches you something! Instead of viewing your failure as a problem, you can use it to learn throughout your entire process of critical thinking and solving the problem.

This process usually continues until a solution is discovered, or you eventually give up, accepting defeat. However, remember that people are seldom really successful in their first attempts toward success in the first place. Think of how many theories are attempted and failed before any are actually deemed acceptable—failure is part of the process and it's okay. Very few successes come without hurdles or roadblocks—otherwise, everyone would be successful.

Chapter 8:

Teaching Your Child to Think Critically

Critical thinking is not just good for you—even your young children can be taught to think critically. When you teach your child to think critically, you set him or her up for success as well. After all, your child will one day be an adult needing to work to earn a living and be in a healthy relationship as well! Therefore, one of the best gifts you can give your child, one of the most important skills that you can emphasize during childhood, is the ability to think critically. This skill will take time and patience to instill, but if you are committed the results are worthy it. You will have a child that is set up to think in ways that are insightful and intelligent and equipped to handle different life aspects.

Benefits of a Critically Thinking Child

Children as well make use of critical thinking in daily tasks. Even playing video games or playing with peers involves the use of critical thinking and problem-solving. Most of the childhood involves learning, and if you want your child to be able to think as an individual, emphasizing that ability early on is crucial.

When you teach your child to think critically, you provide them with a sort of defense mechanism against peer pressure, every parent's nightmare. Peer pressure can cause children to make decisions that they otherwise would not have because they are afraid to say no and be embarrassed. Instead, they find themselves in over their heads and in dangerous situations all because they couldn't find their own voices and speak for themselves. However, when your child becomes a critical thinker, he or she is able to weigh those pros and cons of the behaviors posed to them, and in so doing, your child is more prepared to say no because they know the best decision to make.

However, apart from that, your child will also be more resilient against any rumors on the internet or viral challenges on social media. For example, the Tide Pod challenge in which teenagers were biting laundry soap pods in their mouths to make them explode? Or other challenges involving dangerous behavior, such as inhaling cinnamon, taking selfies in dangerous areas, or otherwise making poor decisions? When you teach your child to think critically, those will obvious be awful decisions. Why risk your health or life for likes on social media?

If critical thinking is propagated early in life, your child will have an easier time relating to other people. You will have equipped the child with the ability to make decisions that are rational, beneficial and helpful and in a way that makes them well adjusted for life.

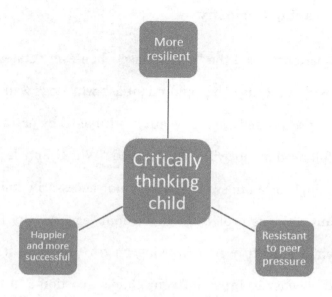

Developing Critical Thinking in Children

Developing critical thinking skills in children does not need to be as intimidating as you may think! It is a matter of a few tweaks on how you approach life, questions and interactions with the child. Just a few changes can be enough to propel your child in the right direction to be the critical thinker that they are capable of.

Encouraging Curiosity

Many parents dread the "why" phase when every statement is laced with curiosity. The child might ask why dogs walk funny, and your response is that they are quadrupedal by nature. They may follow that up with the dreaded "Why?" and leave you scrambling for an answer. You may not necessarily know why so many animals evolved to be on four legs, or why humans happened to shift over to walking on two legs, and it can be incredibly easy to brush off your child's question and tell him that you do not know.

However, these questions are the perfect opportunity to begin developing the critical thinking that your child will need as an adult. Instead of dismissing them, encourage the questions. Encourage your child to think about why they think that dogs walk on four legs instead of two and why humans don't use their hands to walk. You may be surprised—even young children may be able to piece together that if they walked on their fours, they would not possible be able to use their hands well. Encourage creativity, curiosity, follow up on the questions and exploration stage with discovering the answer as well. This helps your child learn to think about theories, experiment and research. When your child is wrong about an answer, you should encourage them to continue thinking about why they may be wrong or how they could change their assumptions to fit better and try again.

Learning from Others

Sometimes, what your child needs is the presence of other sources to answer those questions brewing in their head. If your child is asking you why cars work the way they do and you happen to know a mechanic, for example, encourage your child to call up the mechanic, with your supervision and ask questions, or pay them a visit to talk directly. Do not hesitate to pull in examples from books, videos, the internet, friends, family, or even experts at a museum or a zoo to answer those questions that are hard to figure out. Not only are you encouraging your child to learn how to use resources effectively, you are also teaching your child that it is okay to reach out to others when they need assistance or expert opinions.

Help Evaluate Information

Sometimes, your child may feel overwhelmed with all of the information dumped on him during this process of learning how to think critically, and that is okay. What you can do during these times of feeling overwhelmed is to encourage your child to begin evaluating information. For example, if your child comes home upset one day and tells you that his friend has told him that Santa Claus is not real, you may use this as an opportunity to guide your child through evaluation.

Ask your child what he honestly thinks about that matter. Ask why he thinks that way and why his friend happened to say what he did. Through the process, your child learns to evaluate and compare information. This way they can deduce its meaning and draw a right conclusion.

Promote Learning Interests

Sometimes, you may not be very enthusiastic over your child's most recent obsession, it is still important to encourage those interests. Your child is naturally absorbing all sorts of information, and in encouraging them to pursue their favorite interests they will understand their likes and dislikes. You might find that they are more willing to be engaged in discussion, problem-solving, and experimenting when it is about a topic of interest. As a parent, you need to make it about the child and not how exhausting it will be for you. This is because the child is becoming passionate about learning, and that is a fantastic life skill to develop. Following their lead with their favorite topics ensures that you always have a willing participant when you are trying to teach critical thinking.

Use Problem-Solving Regularly

Guide your child through problem-solving as you talk about it in the process. You want to make sure that your child is able to learn the foundation and master the skill of problem solving.

You can guide your child on problem-solving in instances such as: if your child is upset that there is only one cookie left, but there are two children, you could let the child figure out the best way to fix the problem. Most children would immediately understand the importance of sharing. That way everyone gets a piece of the cookie and no one gets left out. However, if they don't come up to that conclusion on the first attempt, you can guide them through your own questions till they figure it out.

Good Listening Skills and Critical Thinking

It's not enough to encourage your child to develop critical thinking, it is important that other skills are also incorporated in the first place. Particularly important is the ability to actively listen. A child who knows how to listen and understand as opposed to mindlessly obeying is evidently brought up with a foundation of critical thinking. Once you encourage your child to become a good listener, you are helping set your child up to be a fantastic critical thinker.

Think back to how many of the steps in critical thinking were contingent upon being a good listener? Most of the skills go hand in hand with the ability to listen. Therefore, you need to be able to listen in order to to ensure that you understand the argument being presented to you. This means, then, that teaching your child to be a good listener will encourage them to be critical thinkers as well.

Luckily, children are extremely receptive to learning how to listen. In fact, many may listen on their own, especially if they ask a question that is relevant to you. In order to make sure that your child is a good listener, you should lead by example. Always practice what you preach. Your child is going to learn how to be a good listener best if he sees you modeling the behavior. After all, the most influential teacher that your child will ever have is you.

When you want to teach your child to listen, remember that you need to show good listening skills yourself. Encourage your child to listen by first starting and connecting with your child. Make sure that you are able to relate somehow—point out how you really like what he is doing at that moment and then ask if you can have a conversation. You make him feel connected to you when you do this, relating to him, and this means that he is more likely to actively listen to you. This is important—your child learns to be respectful and make a connection with the person they have conversations with.

Explain things to your child in as clear a manner as possible without dumbing it down. Your child will learn to do this, as well. When you are speaking, be direct and clear. Encourage your child to also do the same when he wants your attention. Always reciprocate by respecting their need for attention.

To real hold your child's attention when speaking, encourage them to always maintain eye contact and be a good role model of the same behavior. If you want him to put down the toy when you talk to him, put down your phone when he comes to you. It is only fair and natural for you to respect him the way you expect to be respected as well.

When you do finish speaking to your child, make sure that you always ask if he understands. If he does, ask him to parrot it back to you in his own words to test how well he understands it. If he does not understand, encourage him to ask you questions for clarification.

When you lead your child by example, the child also becomes a greater listener. Putting focus on listening to understand rather than to answer or be obedient, which is a huge shift in thinking abilities. When your child is able to listen to you and repeat back what you said in their own words or even explain meaning it's evident that they are developing critical thinking skills.

Positive Mindset Skills and Critical Thinking

Remember, critical thinking skills involves being able to parse out the negative biases and mindsets in order to have the whole picture and not get blindsided negative thoughts. This means that you are more likely to be a good critical thinker if you can successfully push aside the negative thoughts. After all, a major part of critical thinking is being able to manage and cope with failure—it is a part of the process and only natural. For a child to be a critical thinker they should embrace and uphold a positive mindset.

When you want to encourage your child to be a positive thinker, perhaps the easiest way to do so is through making sure that the child understands that bad things happen sometimes, and it's okay. For instance, if your child messes up his birthday cake, maybe dropping it as it was getting set down on the table, and it gets smudged, you can point out that cake still tastes good, no matter what it looks like, and enjoy it anyway. If your child messes up, you can ask them what to do next time in order fix the problem. You can always point out what your child has learned, and make it a teachable moment. In so doing, pointing out the positives and not focusing on the negatives, will come in handy in the child's life.

Chapter 9:

Quick Thinking Exercises to Boost Critical Thinking Skills

Exercise 1: Improve Comedy

This may seem intimidating especially if you are not comfortable with public speaking. However, putting yourself on the spot in a situation like stand-up comedy, can boost spontaneous thinking skills. This means that you will have no choice but to think quickly about random subjects that you may not have considered. Therefore, your mind will have to work on figuring out the best possible progression quickly, in a lighthearted and low-stakes situation.

If you cannot find such an opportunity, you could try setting up something similar at home with trusted friends or family. Have a bunch of different topics, or use a deck of cards with several topics written on them, and have them drawn at random. After which you will be required to talk about the subject for three minutes and make the group laugh as much as possible.

The group then has to score your performance, or you can have a neutral person judge and do the grading.

At first, this can be difficult, especially if you are shy. The upside is that, you are learning to think fast on your feet. Plus, your mind needs to be exercised just as much as your body does, and this is a fun way to do so.

Exercise 2: Get into a Debate

You could try finding a local debate team or just meeting up with one of your friends that loves to argue. During a debate, someone has to think fast and come up with counter-arguments statements. This is great for critical thinking since it already uses logic and arguments that need fast responses. Being able to quickly organize your thought is an aspect of critical thinking.

However, it is highly recommended that you try to avoid topics that might likely get heated, such as politics or religion. Some of the light hearted topic to discuss include: discussing a movie review or why a certain restaurant is better, this way your relationship won't be ruined due to disagreements. You could even set this up as a weekly arrangement, have everyone come up with new topics and even meet at a new location every time. The practice will be good for everyone, as you spend time with friends and work on your critical thinking skills.

Exercise 3: Play Quick-Thinking Board Games

Games that are designed to make you think, such as quick trivia games that need instant answers after pressing the button or buzzer are great ways of boosting fast thinking skills. You may even choose to race a game show on television come up with answers as quick as possible and exercise the brain.

Ultimately, much of learning to speed up your own mind is done through sheer repetition. The more you exercise your mind, the more likely it is to think fast. The more you practice fast thinking the more capable your brains gets. This is good for critical thinking. After all, thinking on your feet is a skill that can be developed and nurtured like any other skill.

Exercise 4: Timed Writing Sprints

Thinking fast does not only have to only involve your mind. You can also speed up other skills while practicing your quick thinking. For example, you can do timed writing sprints. This involves making it a point to write as much as you can about a new subject every single day. You can use a pencil instead of typing and come up with as much information as you can in the given time.

Every day, find a new subject—you could use a random page online, such as the *I'm feeling lucky* search option on Google or some other method, and then write about what you know about it in three minutes. First you will need to brainstorm as much as you can in those three minutes in order to figure out everything that you possibly know about the topic.

Once you are able to write about it, you may consider extending your writing time to more than 10 minutes. In so doing, you are

98

encouraging your mind to be alert and aware. In a way that allows you to quickly process new information about any topic. Regular practice will not only help your writing speed, either by pen or via typing, but it will also help you learn to up your speeds when it comes to brainstorming.

Chapter 10:

Creative Thinking Exercises to Boost Critical Thinking Skills

Exercise 1: Alternative Solution Methods

Identify a problem that you are having or had recently and think about the solution that can be used. Can you come up with another way of fixing the problem that you had not originally thought about? This is a great way of exercising creative thinking skills. In other words, it is figuring out how to think outside the box about a past or current problem.

Since most issues can be difficult to solve, if you do not know what you are doing. Sometimes you have no choice but to look at things from a creative perspective. This is about looking at the issue from all sides to really understand the best way forward. Even if you may already have a perfectly viable solution, perhaps there is a better one that may be more effective.

Why would it work? Exploring other options helps you become flexible in your thinking. You get to a point where you can address issues with ease because you are used to working with unconventional methods. When the unconventional solutions become easy to invent and configure, then the conventional methods become easier as well.

Exercise 2: Consider the Opposite Position

Find an argument that you have made in the past or a cause that you are truly passionate about. After which, you are going to have to turn that position upside down altogether. You may need to do some research in order to figure out how to creatively turn the position around and take the other. You will have to begin considering perspectives that you may not have otherwise considered, that way you will be figuring out how to become a flexible thinker.

This is probably one of the more difficult exercises, as you will be challenged to come up with an argument that is truly the opposite of what you would normally stand for, and you need to actually support it. However, it also benefits you to begin looking at situations in ways that embrace diversity, making it also useful when it comes to developing critical thinking skills. Even though the idea of supporting something you are not enthusiastic about sounds off, the long term benefits are incredible, especially after trying it out a few times.

Exercise 3: Catastrophic Problem Prompt

Imagine waking up one morning to find that you are not at home —in fact you are lost in a cave with no idea where you are or how to get back home. When you look around, you see all sorts of strange and foreign creatures. At first you think it's a dream. However, you pinch yourself and its reality and you are wide awake. Next to you, there's a short man covered in hair that falls at your knees and is holding a helmet, a small dragon that is incredibly snarky and a tall woman who does not seem to speak English at all. How do you figure out where you are and find your way home?

Turn the above prompt into a writing challenge in which you figure out how to get out of this sudden and unexpected situation. You will be working on your creative thinking skills while also using critical thinking skills, such as problem-solving. Writing may not be your thing or something you care for at all, but it can be incredibly useful when you are attempting to practice your critical thinking skills. When you write a story prompt, such as the above one, you are stuck figuring out how to solve problems that are impossible in real life. Because these problems are entirely impossible in real life, you never would have considered them.

Now, in forcing yourself to write about it, you are attempting to come up with a logical way out of an impossible situation with only the information that has been provided to you. As a bonus, you may develop a nice hobby in writing if you happen to love the process!

Exercise 4: Try a Roleplaying Game

Yes, this may seem counterintuitive, but playing video games can actually help you figure out how to think critically. Despite the common misconception that video games may melt the brains of children, they actually do encourage a wide range of important benefits, such as hand-eye coordination and encouraging cooperation and problem-solving. RPGs, in particular, are notorious for having all sorts of ridiculous puzzles that may require some critical and creative thinking skills.

The RPG you play is not quite as important as you actually dedicate yourself to doing so. Several are paced, so beginners can pick them up if you have never played before. If you are not new to games, you can use this as an excuse to pick up the game and practice—call it your critical thinking training and enjoy! This is an enjoyable way to get in that practice that also makes your work seem like play—because it is! When you play through these games, you will encounter all sorts of puzzles, to varying extents and difficulties. Keep in mind that you may need to scale up or down the difficulty level for yourself.

Chapter 11:

Analytical Thinking Exercises to Boost Critical Thinking Skills

Exercise 1: Brain Games

Brain games are a fantastic way for you to boost your analytical thinking abilities without getting bored in the process. There are several games out there that will boost your analytical skills and improve your ability to think critically. These games, from Sudoku to word puzzles in which you must unscramble words, can help you figure out how best to think analytically about a situation around you, and you do not even need to go out of your way to find them, either.

If you are reading this, you probably have access to the internet on some sort of device. The internet holds a plethora of information just waiting for you to take advantage of, and this includes several apps that are designed to help you develop your ability to think analytically. You can download several apps and spend just 10 minutes a day exercising your brain. As you do so, your capacity for analytical thinking increases. This kind of exercise is as crucial as any other. If you prefer numbers over word games, you could play a game such as Sudoku. If you prefer a word or story game, you could focus on games that are designed around solving mysteries.

Exercise 2: Escape Rooms

This is yet another way to make the process fun, escape rooms can be a great exercise in ensuring that you boost your analytical skills. If you do not know what an escape room is, they are rooms or buildings designed to host a game—you are locked in for a specific amount of time with no escape, and you have a determined amount of time to solve the puzzle to escape. Along the way, you and a group of people will find all sorts of clues that point you one direction or another, and it will be on you to figure out how best to get through.

These rooms are not particularly easy, though they are fun for those who like games and challenges. You will have to figure out the clues, decipher them, and follow their lead while under the pressure of the clock. However, they are quite enjoyable despite the intense pressure, and if this is your idea of a good time, you can gather up a group of friends and go have fun regularly. Of course, these rooms are not always available, depending on your location. Keep in mind that you may need to travel or may not be able to find one. If you can, however, this is a great and fun way to build up those analytical skills, while possibly having a date night at the same time!

Exercise 3: 10 Minute Learning Period

Every day, challenge yourself to learn something new. Whatever you choose, make sure you spend 10 minutes learning as much as possible about it in order to enable your mind to absorb information. Part of being able to analyze comes in the form of the ability to rationalize information quickly and effectively, and sometimes, the best way to do so is through choosing a topic at random and learning as much as you can about it.

Think about it this way—if you have ten minutes to learn everything you need to know about aquariums and how to keep them, what are you going to look at? You need to first analyze the information that you know about aquariums so as to redirect your energy elsewhere. If you do not know the difference between tropical, cold water and saltwater fish, you are probably not going to spend the entire ten minutes reading about the benefits, the different shapes of tanks and whether you want acrylic, glass, or something else. Therefore, you would probably look for a beginner's guide that would broadly explain the relevant information. This is so as to get the general idea down before you start specializing. After all, knowing the difference between acrylic and a glass tank is not going to help you keep a fish alive.

Exercise 4: Try a New Project

Every now and then, when you have the time to spare, try something new. This is a great way to break the monotony daily routine, though you might great benefits in teaching yourself a new skill. For example, if you struggle with multitasking, try learning how to cook a meal that requires plenty of multitasking. You can start with something a bit easier that requires you to cook and prepare two different foods at once, and slowly work your way up.

If you choose a new skill that you have little or no experience in, you are forcing your mind to accommodate. You have no choice but to learn the information as quickly as possible, which will put your mind into analysis mode. You will be focused on learning the important information first, this encourages the analysis of information.

Chapter 12:

Communication Exercises to Boost Critical Thinking Skills

Exercise 1: Learn to Listen Well

Communication is crucial to critical thinking. When you are unable to communicate well, it's hard to put your thoughts in words and think critically. After all, if you cannot clearly hear what someone else is saying, can you really say that you are able to understand them? Can you really give them the deserved attention and consideration if you are not even listening effectively? The answer is no.

This is why learning to listen well is a fantastic way to boost your communication ability, which in turn will boost your critical thinking skills. If you are in the process of learning listen for the purpose of understanding instead of merely replying, the major point of emphasis is to give undivided attention. This means that your phone needs to be away and ensure that you maintain eye contact with the person you are talking to. When you are listening, also maintain eye contact and nod your head occasionally.

This shows that you are focused on the conversation and encourages the other person to keep talking. Therefore, avoid getting distracted by your own desire to reply. No matter how much you think you know what the other person is going to say, listen. You need to listen as if you do not know, even if you are able to infer there exact words. You want to listen to their every word before answering, and you should not get distracted thinking of how best to refute what was said. Allow the other person to have the undivided attention that you would like them to give to you as well.

Exercise 2: "I" Statements

Communication with others can be difficult—there is no doubt about that. However, it can be made worse when you are focused on accusatory language rather than making it clear that you are discussing your own thoughts and feelings. When you focus on attacking the other person instead of explaining your thoughts and opinions, the entire situation becomes emotional. Emotional thinking does not fit well in critical thinking, and because of that, you need to figure out a way to avoid that trap. This means that you cannot be telling your partner, "You make me so angry! Or Why are you so bad at this?" when your partner messes up something that you have been trying to teach him.

Instead, it's better to focus on the "I" statements. When you concentrate on your own feelings and opinions rather how the other person makes you feel, and explain the events objectively and then discussing your interpretation, you remove some of the attack from your tone. For example, if your partner has melted your favorite sweater in the dryer, instead of yelling at him, you would instead want to approach the situation objectively in order to ensure that the situation does not escalate. In fact, you may say, "You know, I feel really upset that my sweater melted in the dryer. Can I show you how to use the dryer the next time you're doing laundry to ensure this doesn't happen again?" In this case, you have not attacked your partner for the mistake but instead pointed out that you wanted to work together to ensure the mistake is not repeated. This shows that you are willing to get over it, and that camaraderie is crucial to a relationship.

In keeping emotions out of the communication, you allow your partner to think critically as well. Your partner may realize that he did mess up and agree after admitting fault rather than getting defensive about the entire situation altogether. This means, that you are able to fix the problem while still encouraging the development of critical thinking skills. As a bonus, you may find that your relationship also improves as well!

Exercise3: Deliberately Blocking Communication

Have you ever attempted to communicate with someone that you could not see or hear? It is time to put that to the test with this third exercise—in this exercise, you will intentionally block off communication in order to see how well you and a partner are able to problem-solve. Both of you be blindfolded and instructed not to speak to each other. There is no need to cover up the ears as well, as you will be following the directions of someone else. With your eyes covered and without being able to speak, you will be asked to complete a series of tasks that will require communication.

For example, one person is handed a ball and told that they need to put it into the box. The other person holds the box, but cannot hear, nor gesture, to the other person that the box is next to him. He also has no idea that the other person is holding the ball in the first place. Without the ability to talk, neither person knows where the ball is, where the box is, or how they are supposed to proceed.

This example is meant to encourage critical thinking in two ways—one, you must problem-solve in order to figure out how best to convey what you need to, when you do not even know where the other person is or how to talk to them, and two, to see how lack of communication can hinder a project or a collaborative effort. When you cannot communicate traditionally, you should figure out another way to do so. If not, the task is largely difficult and nearly impossible.

Exercise 4: Telephone

In school, children used to play a game known as the telephone—this was where you would whisper a word to one person, and they had to pass the message all the way around a circle until it reached the individual that said the word, to begin with. When you try this as an adult, it is a great reminder as a team to not trust gossip that comes down the grapevine.

Especially if you were toward the end of the chain, you might hear something that is entirely unrelated to what the first person who started the chain had said. This is meant to show just how unreliable multiple sources of the same information can be. When you are getting information from someone who knew someone who knew someone who read an article about a person who interviewed a person who experienced something, you are not likely to get the original intent behind the discussion. This is a reminder in critical thinking—always judge your sources firmly and fairly to figure out if it was reliable.

Chapter 13:

Open-Mindedness Exercises to Boost Critical Thinking Skills

Exercise 1: What Would ____ Do?

Sometimes, one of the best ways to remind yourself to practice open-mindedness is to put yourself in someone else's mind. If you are facing a problem that has been incredibly difficult for you to manage, maybe what you need is a new perspective on the problem. Stop and consider what someone you admire would do. This person could be a character that you look up to in your favorite book or television series, or you could ask yourself how your mentor or someone else close to you would handle the problem.

When you start to think about something through the mind of someone else, seeing it through their lens and worldview, you are capable of being more open-minded. You can as well see how different people, from different upbringings and experiences, will approach the same situation and offer various solutions. This is a critical skill to remember—when you are able to view things from another perspective, you may see answers to a problem that you otherwise would have remained blind to. This is because you would not have ever felt the need or desire to think things through in a way that was not aligned with your own values.

Diversity is a good thing—when your thoughts are diverse with several other people's experiences wrapped up into it, you are more likely to get a better result. You are also more likely to find the right answer if you are looking at it from several different perspectives, allowing several differing opinions to come together and leave only the right one to prevail over the others. Because of this sort of clash of information and ideas, you should, at least in theory, be able to discover the best way to tackle the problem.

Exercise 2: Draw a 3

This exercise is a reminder to you or anyone else that despite what you may see in front of you, it is incredibly likely that everyone around you sees it entirely different. This is important to remember when you are considering the way that other people look at the world. In this exercise, you are tasked with drawing a 3 on a piece of paper and placing it onto a table in front of you. Next, look at it for a moment—you see a 3, right? Now, move over to another side of the table. What do you see?

As you walk around the table, circling around it, you will notice the change based on the angle you are looking at it from. From one angle, you may see a 3, but from another, it may look like a stylized E. Another angle may show you a W while another looks like an M.

As you move around the table, remember that one thing can have different views. You may see one side of the conflict, but to someone else, it is entirely different. Keep in mind—you will never see the same thing as someone else in a situation, and that is okay. This just means that you can never assume that your views are similar to someone else's and keeping an open mind is crucial.

Exercise 3: Try Something New

Yes, this has already been mentioned before, but this time it is a slightly different context. If you have a partner or a friend who has a hobby or interest that does not line up with your own, now is the time to rope them into the situation as well. You want to expose yourself to something new that you would not normally do. If you have a friend who loves *Dungeons & Dragons*: Try playing for a day to see how it goes. If you normally reject eating Thai food because the smell is too strong: Go with someone else to their favorite Thai restaurant and order their favorite food. If you typically hate a certain genre of movie that your partner loves: Watch a movie that they love with them and try to enjoy it.

As you try something new, ensure that you are trying to understand the reason as to why the other person likes it, also and challenge yourself by saying three nice things about the activity you have just tried. Even if Thai food is not your thing or you hated the movie say three things that you appreciate and are worth mentioning.

When you do this, you will get a chance to gain new experiences and might even like it. Appreciating that others having an opposing viewpoint on something from you is a great way to really open your mind and tackle any biases you may have had. You might not like Thai food still, but you can at least see what your friend sees in it, and that is important.

Exercise 4: Go Somewhere New

No, you do not have to take a vacation to some faraway land— though you are more than welcome to do so. You do not even need to leave town to complete this exercise. When you go somewhere new, somewhere you have never been to. Even within a single town, you may realize that things are quite divided. Even today, it is totally normal to see certain income brackets or races sort of segregated and others maintaining some distance.

This means, that you it's possible to find areas that you are not familiar with in your own town. By going to an unfamiliar and observing the homes, the way the yard is cared for and the people you can understand their way of life. Of course, this is not to say that you can walk through a neighborhood full of predominantly lower-income individuals and pretend you suddenly understand them—but you can open your eyes to their ways of life. You may see that there are windows boarded up that have been broken, or cars that look like they have seen better days. If you have spent most of your life in a wealthier neighborhood, you are not likely going to realize that there are people living so differently, not too far away from where you are.

However, while doing this, you should make sure that you are always respectful and open-minded. The purpose of this is to make sure that you see how people from the same town can have diverse upbringing either better or worse.

Chapter 14:

Problem Solving Exercises to Boost Critical Thinking Skills

Exercise 1: "To-Do" Scavenger Hunt

This is best done in a group of people, such as in a classroom or with other people around. You must set up a series of challenges that are then expected to be done in groups, allowing everyone to work toward the same end goal. First, start out with groups of people and randomized tasks, but if you are by yourself, you can also do so by setting up several dozen random problem-solving exercises and then drawing out six every time you challenge yourself to this. Each of the problems that are included should be something relatively simple but requiring some sort of problem-solving skills.

For example, maybe you challenge yourself to write a poem about one specific theme. This theme could randomly be anything, and it has to rhyme, with the first words provided.

Perhaps the first line of the poem must end in *"Yellow,"* and every other line must rhyme with it, all about the topic of winter.

Another example could be a dare to drink an entire glass of liquid without spilling it—without your hands and without a straw. You then need to figure out a way to accomplish this.

As you can see, the problems that must be solved do not need to be serious problems—presenting them as games can actually make the problem-solving much more enjoyable. While doing this alone, encourage yourself to think outside the box in low-stakes environments. As a bonus, if you do this in a group, it can be fun to watch people try to solve these together!

Exercise 2: Will it Float?

In this exercise, you and a group of people, if you have anyone around that can help you with this, are tasked with coming up with some sort of floating game with only the items that you can get your hands on in 30 seconds. When you are ready to begin, someone sets off a 30-second timer, and everyone is off to gather their objects. The task at hand is to create some sort of raft that will allow for a paperclip to float atop a body of water. The teams or groups are given 5 minutes to complete the challenge.

This particular exercise brings two skills to the table: Not only do you require to think critically but you are also pushing yourself to work in with a team. This means that you have to use several other critical thinking skills, such as good communication and ensuring that you are listening to all the instruction in the race.

Exercise 3: A Marble Run—with a Twist

In this exercise, you are challenged to come up with a marble run. If you have children, you may already have a kit for this. However, you need to set up a marble run that will trigger something. Your marble run must be used to put out a candle that is placed on a table. Of course, you must be mindful of danger when doing this—make sure that you are applying the right fire safety skills and do not burn down the room that you are doing the challenge in. However, beyond that, the only limit here is your imagination.

While you do this challenge, you must figure out how to use a marble run to trigger a reaction that will extinguish the candle. There are several different ways of doing this—you could have a cup fall upside-down over the candle or try having water spilled on the candle at the end of the marble run or you could even use the marble run to turn on a fan that blows it out.

No matter the method that you choose, what matters is that you are able to drop the marble in the beginning and have the candle blown out. Good luck!

This is meant to have you thinking critically and creatively—you have a task at hand that is blowing out the candle somehow, and the method to do so—using a marble run. How can you, or even a group of people, figure out how best to use the marble run to cause the candle to go out? This can be tricky to figure out at first, but once you do it, you will find that marble runs, despite being designed for children, can be quite fun.

Exercise 4: The Spaghetti Bridge

Perhaps meant for children while teaching them the art of critical thinking, this last exercise is about making some sort of bridge using straight spaghetti noodles and anything else that you can find to create a bridge that will stand while small die-cast cars are driven over it. The trick here is to ensure that the bridge is able to withstand the weight and remain intact.

Particularly for children, this can be exciting—dry pasta is not exactly notorious for being particularly difficult to snap. Nevertheless, when you use this method, you are working together to figure out how to solve the problem, and having fun while at it.

Conclusion

Congratulations! You have made it to the end of *Critical Thinking*. Hopefully, you have found this book as informative, useful, and actionable as it was intended to be. When you made it a point to choose this book and read, you dedicated yourself to learning how to think in a way that was critical, perhaps not knowing the benefits that would come along with it. Critical thinking is crucial to success in this day and age, both for adults and children alike, and when you make it a point to develop your own critical thinking abilities, you will realize that you are much happier than before.

Critical thinking itself, as you have learned, comes with several benefits. When you can think critically, you are able to communicate better, which promotes better relationships with others. This leads to more happiness and fulfillment. With the ability to think critically, you can identify solutions to problems that you did not realize were as difficult to solve as they were, and you are rarely giving up.

Critical thinkers utilize their abilities constantly—you can figure out how to make your decisions, how to interact with others, and why you should think or act in a certain manner all because you learned how to think critically. You learned how to consider situations around you in ways that are deliberate, attentive to detail, meticulous, and meant to bring you closer to solving any problems that you encounter. On top of that, always managing to make your way to the right decision, even if you encounter some roadblocks along the way. Nevertheless, when you become a critical thinker, one thing is for sure: You become more intelligent, informed and capable of making judgments that are trustworthy and valuable.

From here, you have several options such as: continuing to work on understanding your own critical thinking abilities, looking into the development of emotional intelligence, another soft skill that is quite closely related to critical thinking, begin working on the exercises that were provided in the last section of this book to develop your own critical thinking abilities, choosing to take classes on the subject, read into philosophy, or other schools of thought that require critical thinking to be at the forefront of your mind. No matter what it is that you choose to do, you can do so with confidence.

If you choose to pursue critical thinking skills for your child, you may decide to find a child-specific critical thinking book in order to begin developing a list of activities that you can do with your child to develop his or her own critical thinking capacity. If that is the path that you take, know that you are giving your child a great opportunity and a tool that will serve him or her well in life, thanks to your willingness to put in the effort and instill these skills.

No matter what you choose to do with this information, good luck on your future endeavors. You now have the skills that you will need to see it to fruition with the steps provided in how to think critically. As you go off on your own, thank you once again for taking the time to read this book. If you have found this book to be useful to you at all, please feel free to leave a review on Amazon. Your feedback and honest opinions are always appreciated and greatly welcomed! Good luck once more and thank you for letting me join you in this process!

CPSIA information can be obtained
at www.ICGtesting.com
Printed in the USA
BVHW051009070921
616217BV00002B/66